The Science of Living Things

What is a Rodent?

Bobbie Kalman & Jacqueline Langille

Crabtree Publishing Company

www.crabtreebooks.com

The Science of Living Things Series
A Bobbie Kalman Book

To Catherine, Sebastian, and Olivier

Editor-in-Chief
Bobbie Kalman

Writing team
Bobbie Kalman
Jacqueline Langille

Managing editor
Lynda Hale

Project editor
Heather Levigne

Editing team
Niki Walker
Hannelore Sotzek
John Crossingham

Copy editor
Jane Lewis

Computer design
Lynda Hale
Trevor Morgan (cover type)

**Production coordinator
and photo researcher**
Hannelore Sotzek

Consultant
K. Diane Eaton, Hon. B.Sc., B.A., Brock University

Photographs
Bobbie Kalman: pages 8 (bottom), 11, 24
Diane Majumdar: front cover
Robert McCaw: pages 4, 8-9, 10, 12, 20, 23 (both)
Photo Researchers, Inc.: Tom McHugh: pages 17 (top), 18,
    Thierry Van Baelinghem: page 31
Roger Rageot/David Liebman: page 14
James H. Robinson: page 27 (bottom)
James P. Rowan: pages 3, 19
Tom Stack & Associates: Nancy Adams: page 30; Dominique
    Braud: pages 26, 29; Jeff Foott: page 25; Thomas Kitchin:
    title page, pages 5, 22, 27 (top); Joe McDonald: page 28;
    Joe and Carol McDonald: pages 13 (bottom), 16; Brian
    Parker: page 30 (top); Dave Watts: page 13 (top)
Other images by Digital Stock and Eyewire, Inc.

Illustrations
Barbara Bedell: back cover, pages 6-7, 9, 15 (top), 21, 29
Jeannette McNaughton-Julich: pages 11, 25

Separations and film
Dot 'n Line Image Inc.

Printer
Worzalla Publishing Company

Crabtree Publishing Company

www.crabtreebooks.com   1-800-387-7650

Cataloging in Publication Data
Kalman, Bobbie
    What is a rodent?

(The science of living things)
Includes index.

ISBN 0-86505-923-3 (library bound)   ISBN 0-86505-951-9 (pbk.)
This book describes the main types of rodents and their physiology, habitats,
behavior, diet, and offspring. 1. Rodents—Juvenile literature. [1. Rodents.] I.
Langille, Jacqueline. II. Title. III. Series: Kalman, Bobbie. Science of living things.
QL737.R6K285 1999   J599.35   LC 99-25867
                                                    CIP

**Published in
the United States**
PMB16A
350 Fifth Ave.
Suite 3308
New York, NY
10118

**Published
in Canada**
616 Welland Ave.
St. Catharines, Ontario
Canada
L2M 5V6

**Published in the
United Kingdom**
White Cross Mills
High Town, Lancaster
LA1 4XS
United Kingdom

**Published
in Australia**
386 Mt. Alexander Rd.
Ascot Vale (Melbourne)
VIC 3032

Contents

What is a rodent?

Rodents are **mammals**. Like most mammals, rodents have fur and a backbone. All mammals are **warm-blooded**—their body can adjust so that its temperature stays the same in hot or cold surroundings. Female mammals are the only animals that make milk in their body to feed their babies.

Some rodents, such as this groundhog, enjoy basking in the sun.

Terrific teeth

Rodents are the only mammals with teeth that never stop growing. They have four front teeth that grow throughout their life. Rodents use their teeth to chew on hard objects such as nuts or tree bark. They can chew through almost anything, from wooden boxes to sheets of metal. Some rodents even use their teeth as tools for digging.

Most rodents do not have white teeth. Some, such as this porcupine, have bright orange teeth. Others have brown or yellow teeth.

The rodent family tree

Rodents are the largest group of mammals. There are more than 1700 **species**, or kinds, of rodents. The pygmy jerboa is the smallest. It is only six inches (15 cm) long, and four (10 cm) of those inches are the length of its tail! The capybara is the largest rodent. It can grow to be five feet (1.5 m) long.

Rodents are grouped into three categories: **squirrel-jawed rodents**, **mouse-jawed rodents**, and **porcupine-jawed rodents**. The rodents in each group have similar teeth and jaws.

springhare

Squirrel-jawed rodents
Squirrel-jawed rodents include beavers, muskrats, squirrels, springhares, pocket gophers, scaly-tailed squirrels, pocket mice, and kangaroo rats.

North American beaver

red squirrel

Mouse-jawed rodents

Mouse-jawed rodents include rats, mice, voles, gerbils, jerboas, hamsters, lemmings, dormice, jumping mice, birch mice, and North African mole-rats.

gerbil

rat

jerboa

Porcupine-jawed rodents

Porcupine-jawed rodents include porcupines, cavies, capybaras, gundis, South African mole-rats, domestic guinea pigs, chinchillas, agoutis, and nutrias.

North American porcupine

chinchilla

capybara

A rodent's body

Every rodent, big or small, has large, strong, curved teeth called **incisors**—two in the center of the upper jaw and two in the center of the lower one. Many rodents have stretchy cheek pouches that they fill with food. They carry the food back to their nest in these pouches.

Some rodents can turn their ears in the direction of a sound to hear it better.

A rodent uses its whiskers to feel its way around in the dark.

A rodent's excellent sense of smell helps it find food that is buried underground or hidden away.

Most rodents have sharp claws. Some dig holes with their claws, and others use them to climb trees.

Rodents often use their front paws like hands. They use them to pick up and hold onto food while they chew.

Most rodents are born with no fur. They grow fur as they become adults. A few types, however, do not grow any fur.

Some rodents have a thick, bushy tail; some have a flat, scaly tail, and others have no tail at all!

What big teeth you have!

A rodent's incisors never stop growing, so the animal must wear them down by rubbing them together and chewing on tough foods. If a rodent does not grind its teeth, the top incisors could curve back and pierce the rodent's skull. Gnawing also sharpens the teeth's **enamel**, causing them to become chisel-shaped.

At home in any habitat

Every type of **habitat** is home to at least one species of rodent. A habitat is the natural place where plants or animals live. Rodents live in trees, on the ground, and underground. They build homes in marshes, forests, prairies, and cities.

A comfortable home

Rodents need a safe, dry **den**, or shelter, where they can sleep, store food, hide from enemies, and raise their babies. Desert rodents use their underground den to escape the sun and stay cool. Those living in cold habitats need their den for warmth. Rodent homes can be as simple as a nest of grass or as complex as a series of underground tunnels.

Finding a home

Rodents do not always build their own home. Some search for a ready-made den. Certain squirrels, for example, move into natural hollows in trees. Others use abandoned woodpecker nesting holes for their den. Mice and rats often chew through walls in buildings and make their nests in the space between the boards.

Living underground

To protect themselves, many rodents make their home in underground dens. Prairie dogs dig separate living rooms and food-storage rooms that are joined by long tunnels. Chipmunks dig **burrows**, or holes, in the forest floor. They often hide the entrance under a log. In fields, woodchucks dig two entrances for their den. One opening is a spy hole that the animal uses to check for danger.

Almost all rodents build a nest inside their den. They use any soft materials they find, such as grass, leaves, or feathers.

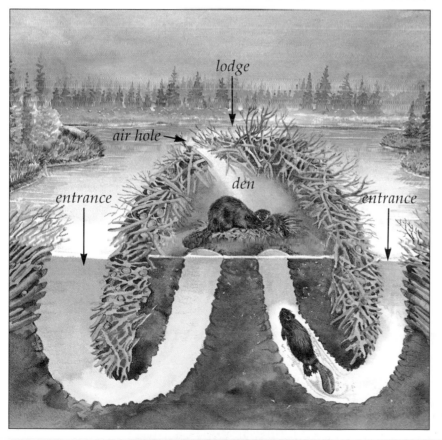

lodge

air hole

den

entrance

entrance

Lodge members

Beavers spend most of their time in water, but they need a dry area for resting. They build a shelter called a **lodge** in which they form their den. Some dig their lodge in a riverbank. The dome-shaped lodge shown in this picture is made of branches, small trees, and mud. It is in the middle of a river. The den can be reached only through two underwater entrances. Inside the den, the beavers are safe from **predators**. To let in fresh air, the animals make an air hole at the top of the lodge.

All about mice

Mice live in nearly every kind of habitat including forests, deserts, and marshes. A few species nest in trees and rarely go down to the ground. In cold areas, mice survive the winter in tunnels under the snow. Many mice live near humans in barns, houses, and other buildings.

A popular meal

Mice are an important part of many **food chains**. Food chains are made up of plants and animals that eat one another to survive. Mice eat plants, and many predators eat mice. Animals that eat mice include wolves, cats, toads, foxes, owls, and snakes.

They'll eat almost anything!

Most rodents are **herbivores**. Herbivores eat mainly plants. Many types of mice, however, eat insects as well as seeds, nuts, and fruit. Animals that eat other animals as well as plants are called **omnivores**.

Many mice

Mice, like most rodents, have large families to help their species survive. Female mice usually have **litters** of ten to 24 **pups**, or babies, at a time. Some species of mice have litters more than four times a year. Baby mice grow up quickly and are often ready to start their own families when they are only six weeks old.

(above) Mice eat almost anything, including soap and wallpaper glue. These "foods" provide protein and fat. Most mice do not eat a lot of cheese!

(below) Pups are born blind and helpless. This deer mouse protects her pups until they are old enough to leave the nest.

Aw, rats!

Rats look like mice, but they are larger and have a pointed snout, which is the front part of their head. There are more than 500 types of rats. Black and brown rats are found almost all over the world. Rats spread diseases and destroy crops, so many people do not like them. In some areas, however, rats are so common that people eat them as a regular part of their diet.

Night dwellers

Most rats are **nocturnal**, which means they are active mainly at night. They rest during the day and come out when the sun sets. In the dark, rats are able to hide easily from predators such as snakes and owls. Most rats, however, cannot see well in the dark. They use their sensitive whiskers and strong sense of smell to help them locate food and find their way around.

Living with people

Rats usually live wherever there are people. Rats live near people because they can find food easily in houses, barns, warehouses, and granaries. They do not like cold temperatures, so they make their nest in buildings. In some areas, people have taken over the habitats of many of the rat's natural predators such as foxes. With more buildings in which to live and fewer predators to threaten them, rats have increased in number.

Kangaroo rats live in deserts. Their body conserves water, or uses so little, that their urine is as dry as powder.

Rats made their way from Europe to North America aboard ships that carried settlers and supplies.

Dozens of cousins

Mice and rats have many relatives such as voles, lemmings, and hamsters. To tell the difference between one type of mouselike rodent and another, look at the tail. Mice and rats have a long tail that is the same length as their body. Voles have a short tail that is one to two inches (3 to 5 cm) long. A lemming's tail is less than an inch (2 cm) long, and a hamster's tail is even shorter.

Tunneling voles

In order to survive, voles must eat close to their own weight in food each day. They spend most of their time looking for food. When searching, voles make tunnels, called **runways**, through the tall grass. They leave trails of urine so that they can follow the scent back to their den. In winter, they tunnel under the snow.

If all the young from one pair of meadow voles lived to have babies, and those babies lived to have babies, there would be one million voles at the end of a year!

Lemmings on the loose

Lemmings live in a cold desert area called the **tundra**. People rarely see them in their habitat. Every few years, however, a **lemming year** occurs. At this time, large groups of lemmings **migrate**, or travel, to a new place to find more food. Many die as they try to climb down cliffs or swim across oceans in search of a new home.

When a lemming feels threatened, it does not run from an enemy. Instead, it rolls onto its back and tries to bite and scratch its attacker!

Storing food

Hamsters eat mainly plants such as grass, clover, grain, and vegetable roots, but they also eat frogs, lizards, earthworms, and small birds and mice. Most wild hamsters store food in a **hoard**. Inside their burrow, they dig a hole in which they put food that they will eat during the winter, when less food is available.

Furry friends

Hamsters are popular pets. Unlike larger animals, hamsters do not need a lot of space. They need only a clean cage with wood shavings on the floor and enough room to build a nest. They also need fresh water and food to stay healthy.

Many children keep hamsters as pets because these small animals are easy to care for.

Jerboas and gerbils

Jerboas and gerbils live mainly in dry desert habitats from Africa to central Asia. They are able to survive in such hot places because they spend the day in cool underground burrows. Jerboas and gerbils come out only at night when it is much cooler.

Thirst quenchers

Jerboas and gerbils hardly ever drink water because it is difficult to find in their habitat. They get the water they need by eating the juicy parts of plants, seeds, and insects.

Jerboas JUMP!

Jerboas have hind legs that are at least four times as long as their front legs. Long hind legs help make them great jumpers. Some jerboas can leap ten feet (3 m) with one jump! Jerboas spend most of their time standing upright on their hind legs. They use their long tail for balance.

Jerboas mainly use their front feet to pick up and hold onto their food. When a jerboa moves slowly, however, it hops like a rabbit, putting its front paws on the ground for balance.

Now you see me...

Gerbils can jump almost as well as jerboas, but they prefer to run. They often stop to sit up on their long hind feet and look around. Gerbils rely on their **camouflage** to hide them from predators. Camouflage is the coloring or markings on an animal's body that help the animal blend in with its surroundings. A gerbil's fur coat is almost the same color as sand. When the gerbil stands still, it is difficult for predators to see it.

Gerbils were brought to North America in 1954 for scientific studies. Scientists took some of the gerbils home as pets for their children. Those gerbils had babies that eventually became pets in other homes. Gerbils are still popular pets today.

Life in the trees

Tree squirrels and flying squirrels are the "acrobats" of the rodent world. They live high above the ground, climbing, running, and leaping among trees. Their body is suited to their tree-dwelling life. A squirrel's feet have long claws for hooking onto rough surfaces such as bark, and its back toes can bend and grip branches.

A tool for a tail

Squirrels have a bushy tail. A tree squirrel's tail is an important tool. When jumping between trees, squirrels use their tail for balance. It also provides shade from the sun or shelter from rain. In cold weather, squirrels wrap their thick tail around their body for warmth.

Scatter-hoarding

Squirrels hoard food for the winter, but they do not store it all in one place. Instead, they **scatter-hoard**, or bury single nuts in many places, all over their territory. Squirrels continually return to the same places and use **landmarks**, or the features of a particular area, to help them find their hoards.

A squirrel always comes down a tree headfirst so that it can see where it is going and watch for predators.

Flying squirrels

Flying squirrels do not really fly. They glide from a high point to a lower one using their **patagia**. Patagia are thin, fur-covered flaps of skin that extend from the front leg to the rear leg on each side of the squirrel's body. To glide, the squirrel spreads its limbs and stretches its patagia to make a wide, kitelike surface. It then jumps into the air, using its legs and tail to steer itself as it glides.

Baby flying squirrels need to practice landing on upright surfaces such as tree trunks.

Squirrels are among the few mammals that can scatter-hoard food and remember where it is. A dog is another type of mammal that can scatter-hoard.

At home on the ground

Some squirrel-jawed rodents rarely climb trees. They are called ground squirrels. They dig burrows in the soil and search for food on the ground. Woodchucks and chipmunks are two common types of ground squirrels. Woodchucks are also known as whistle pigs, groundhogs, and marmots.

Sleeping the winter away

Woodchucks do not hoard their food. They eat plenty of food in the summer and early fall to build up their body fat. During the winter, woodchucks **hibernate**, or go into a type of long, deep sleep.

When an animal hibernates, it uses little energy. It hardly breathes, its heart beats very slowly, and its body temperature cools. Its fat provides all the **energy** it needs. When warm weather returns, the animal wakes up and searches for a meal.

The Arctic ground squirrel hibernates for seven months of the year because it lives on the cold tundra of Alaska and northern Canada.

It's Groundhog Day!

In North America, February 2 is called Groundhog Day. There is a **myth** that hibernating woodchucks wake up to check the weather. If the sun is shining and the woodchuck sees its shadow, it becomes frightened and hurries back into its burrow to sleep. If the groundhog returns to sleep, people say that there will be six more weeks of winter. If it is cloudy, the groundhog cannot see its shadow so it stays awake, which means winter is almost finished. In reality, most woodchucks hibernate well past Groundhog Day.

Living alone

Some rodents live in large family groups for most of their life. Most chipmunks, however, live alone. When two chipmunks meet at a favorite feeding area, each bares its teeth to scare away the other. If neither leaves, they fight—biting and scratching each other until one flees. Male and female chipmunks get together only to produce babies. The mother chipmunk spends six to eight weeks with her young before they go off to live alone.

Champion diggers

Prairie dogs and gophers have bodies that are built for digging. They have powerful front legs and strong claws. Their long, strong incisors help loosen packed soil and can cut through roots. These rodents have lips that close tightly behind their incisors to keep out dirt while they dig. Their eyes release a fluid that clears away dirt and dust.

*Prairie dogs are **social** animals, which means they spend most of their time together. Prairie dogs use touch and smell to identify members of their group.*

Prairie-dog towns

Prairie dogs build underground tunnels for their homes. A family of prairie dogs, called a **coterie**, builds its home near the homes of other families. Soon, a **prairie-dog town** is formed. Some towns cover as much land as a city block!

Helping the environment

When rodents build their underground home, they also help nature. Digging mixes air into the dirt, which helps plants grow. Rodent droppings and plants left underground **fertilize**, or add nutrients to, the soil. Fertile soil produces more plants, providing more food for rodents and other animals.

*In summer, burrows provide a cool place for prairie dogs to escape the hot sun. In winter, these rodents stay warm inside their burrow because the air is very **humid**, or warm and damp.*

What's in your pockets?

Pocket gophers have two long, fur-lined side pouches on the outside of their face. The pouches stretch from the sides of their face back to their shoulders. These pouches hold large amounts of food. When they get dirty, a gopher is able to turn them inside out to clean them!

*Pocket gophers are **fossorial**, which means they are suited to burrowing underground. They live in tunnels and dig out plant roots to eat. Sometimes they go to the surface to gather food to store in their burrow.*

Water lovers

All rodents can swim if necessary, but some types spend most of their time in the water. Muskrats, beavers, and nutrias make their homes in or near water. Their bodies are suited to life in the water. Beavers and nutrias have webbed feet for paddling through the water. Muskrats and beavers have a wide, flat tail to help them steer as they swim.

Dam builders

Beavers are the "lumberjacks" of the rodent family. Using their strong incisors as a chisel, beavers are able to cut down trees. They use logs and branches to build **dams** across rivers and streams. The dams trap the water and cause it to **flood**, or overflow, forming a pond. Beavers use this pond as a place to build their lodge and escape from predators.

The perfect depth

Muskrats eat mainly bottom-growing water plants. The water in which they live must be shallow enough for water plants to grow. If it is too deep, sunlight will not reach the plants on the bottom. The water also must be deep enough so that it does not freeze to the bottom in winter or dry up in summer.

Waterproof rodents

Nutrias and beavers live by rivers and in swamps. Their soft fur is covered by long, rough **guard hairs**. **Glands** near their mouth secrete an oily substance that they spread over their fur to help keep water away from their skin.

(above) A muskrat uses its teeth to carry food to the surface of the water. It eats on a floating platform that it builds out of plants.

Nutrias were first brought from South America to North America by farmers who raised them for their fur. Some nutrias escaped from the farms and had babies in the wild.

Capybaras

Capybaras are the largest rodents. Some weigh more than 100 pounds (45 kg)! They live in large **herds**, or groups, of 20 to 40 animals. Their habitat is the wet, grassy areas of South America. Capybaras are herbivores that eat mainly grass. Their name, in fact, means "master of the grass." A capybara's feet are webbed, and it can swim almost as well as beavers, nutrias, and muskrats.

Dangers to capybaras

In some areas, the capybara population is decreasing. Wetlands are drained to clear land for farming and building, so many capybaras have nowhere to live. Others are hunted for their fur and meat. Some people, however, are trying to help the capybaras. These people are raising them on ranches in order to help increase their numbers.

Get my point?

Porcupines live high among the trees and are skilled climbers. Strong claws and small, rough knobs on their feet allow porcupines to grip tree trunks. Some porcupines have short, stiff hairs on the underside of their tail to help brace their body against the tree as they climb.

Prickly quills

Three types of hair cover a porcupine's body—short underfur, long guard hairs, and hard, sharp quills. When a baby porcupine is born, its quills are damp and soft. Within hours, however, the quills dry and harden, becoming sharp and dangerous.

Get away from me!

Quills help protect the porcupine from enemies. A porcupine swings its prickly tail to defend itself. As the tail strikes the predator, the quills come off. Tiny **barbs**, or hooks, make the quills stick in the predator's body. Every time the animal moves, the quills go deeper into its skin. Some predators die when a porcupine quill pierces their heart or brain.

Porcupines rely on trees for safety as well as food. They strip off the bark with their sharp teeth.

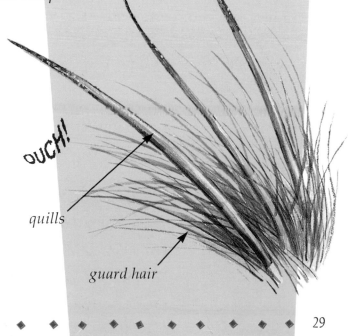

OUCH!

quills

guard hair

29

More relatives

Other members of the porcupine-jawed rodent group include agoutis, cavies, maras, and chinchillas. Most of these rodents live in South America.

Who are you calling a pig?

A guinea pig is not actually a pig but a rodent. This rodent has lived with people for centuries. The Incas, a group of Native people in South America, raised guinea pigs for food and as pets. Like the Incas, many people today find guinea pigs to be lovable pets. In North America and Europe, guinea pigs also have been used in testing cures for diseases.

I've got an agouti!

Agoutis live in rain forests, where they can hide from predators among the plants and trees. There is one easy way to find an agouti, though—toss pebbles into the air! When the small objects fall to the ground, they make a sound like that of nuts or small fruits falling from trees. Nuts and fruits are an agouti's favorite food, so when the animal hears the sound, it runs out of its den in hope of finding a snack!

(above) Guinea pigs use a whistling noise to communicate with one another.

(below) Agoutis run quickly through their forest habitat. If they cannot escape their enemies by hopping and running through bushes, they jump into nearby water and swim away.

Fabulous fur

Of all the fur-bearing rodents in the world, chinchillas have the thickest and softest coat. Their fur provides them with protection from the cold weather in their mountain habitat. For many years, people hunted chinchillas for their luxurious coat. The beauty of their fur almost caused these animals to become **extinct**. When an animal is extinct, it is gone forever.

Chinchillas eat mainly fruits and plants, such as grasses, leaves, bark, and a few types of cactus.

Words to know

burrow (n) An animal's underground home; (v) to dig underground

coterie A prairie dog family

dam A barrier made of sticks and mud, used to stop the flow of water and create a pond

enamel The hard outer layer of a tooth

energy The power needed to do things

extinct Describing a species of animal or plant that no longer exists

food chain A pattern of eating and being eaten; for example, a plant is eaten by a mouse, which is then eaten by a snake

fossorial Describing an animal that is suited to living underground

gland A body part that releases a substance

guard hair A long hair used to protect an animal's soft underfur

herbivore An animal that eats mainly plants

hibernate To go into a heavy sleep during the winter months

hoard (n) A store of food; (v) to store food

incisor A front tooth used for gnawing

litter A group of babies born at one time to an animal

migrate To move from one place to another in search of food or shelter

myth A story that is made up to explain unusual events

omnivore An animal that eats both plants and animals

predator An animal that hunts and eats other animals

prey An animal that is hunted and eaten by another animal

semi-desert Describing an area that has little rainfall and few plants

social Describing animals that live in groups

species A group of very similar living things whose offspring can make babies

tundra A cold, dry, treeless area that has frozen soil

Index

6 7 8 9 0   Printed in the U.S.A.   8 7 6